The Gre
Butter Cookbook

Every recipe a peanut butter lover
needs!

Table of Contents

Introduction

Peanut Butter is one of those amazing ingredients that needs to be used more often. There is so much rich, nutty flavor packed into peanut butter and this cookbook is ready to take full advantage of all peanut butter has to offer. So, forget the boring old peanut butter and jelly sandwich, we have so much more for you! With this awesome cookbook, you can bake, drink, marinate, and dip with peanut butter all with some great easy to follow recipes. Are you getting excited? I know I am!

I wrote this cookbook because I absolutely love peanut butter and wanted to share all the creative ways to use it in cooking. Besides its fantastic tastes and versatility, I love that peanut butter is not an expensive ingredient. For just a little money, you get so much! One jar of peanut butter can give you peanut butter toffee cookies (one of my personal favorite recipes), some peanut butter salad dressing and a peanut butter milkshake! Sounds like a great assortment to me! While most of my recipe ask for smooth peanut butter, you can definitely use chunky as well in recipes like the super fudgey peanut butter brownies or the carnival bananas- any recipe where you won't mind a crunch!

If you have a nice jar of peanut butter handy, then it's time to get started on your first recipe! Maybe begin with the peanut butter mocha latte to give you a nice energy boost and then get baking some peanut butter dog treats- you don't want to deprive anyone from delicious peanut butter!!

Peanut Butter Toffee Cookies

These amazing cookies combine the classic peanut butter cookie with toffee pieces making them hard to resist. If you love peanut butter cookies, then these are sure to be your new favorite!

Yield: 24 Cookies

Time: 30 minutes

Ingredients:

- 1 cup butter
- 1 1/4 cup Peanut Butter
- 1 cup Sugar
- 1 cup Brown Sugar
- 2 Eggs
- 2 1/2 cup Flour
- 1 teaspoon Baking Powder
- 1/2 teaspoon Salt
- 1 teaspoon Vanilla
- 1 cup Toffee pieces

Directions:

- In a mixer with a paddle attachment, mix the butter, peanut butter, sugar and brown sugar until fluffy and light, scraping down the bowl several times
- Add the eggs and vanilla and scrape the bowl down again, making sure everything is thoroughly mixed.

- Add all the dry ingredients to the bowl and mix until a dough forms.
- Add the toffee pieces to the dough and mix until combined
- Scoop cookie dough onto a greased cookie sheet about 2 inches apart and bake in a 350 F oven for 1012 minutes or until the edges start to brown. Cool and Enjoy!

Peanut Butter Cup Cookie Cups

A peanut butter cookie wrapped around a peanut butter cup I'll take 2 please! These little delicacies make dessert even better I mean, cookies and candy! You can't go wrong!

Yield: 36 cookies

Time: 40 minutes

Ingredients:

- 1 1/4 cup Flour
- 3/4 teaspoon Baking Soda
- 3/4 teaspoon Salt
- 1/2 cup butter
- 1/2 cup Peanut Butter
- 1 cup Brown Sugar
- 1 egg
- 2 teaspoons Vanilla Extract
- 36 mini peanut butter cups, unwrapped

Directions:

- In a mixer with a paddle attachment, cream the butter, peanut butter and brown sugar until fluffy and light.
- Add the eggs and vanilla and scrape down the sides of the bowl to make sure the butter is fully incorporated.
- Add the flour, baking soda and salt and mix until the dough comes together.

- Scoop the dough and roll into 1 1/2 inch balls and place the balls in a miniature muffin pan one cookie dough ball per muffin cup.
- Press the peanut butter cup into the center of the cookie ball. The cookie dough should come up around the peanut butter cup but be level with the top on the peanut butter cup.
- Bake in a 350°F oven for about 10 minutes. Allow to cool before removing the cookies from the pan.

Chocolate Peanut Butter Buttercream

The brown color of this frosting may look like just chocolate but take a bit and the peanut butter flavor will fill your mouth! A perfect combination of chocolate and peanut butter it doesn't get any better!

Yield: Frosting for 24 cupcakes or one 6" Cake

Active Time: 15 minutes

Ingredients:

- 1 cup Butter
- 1 cup Peanut Butter
- 1/2 cup Cream Cheese
- 4 Tablespoons Milk
- 4 cups Powdered Sugar
- 2 teaspoons Vanilla
- 1/4 teaspoon Salt
- 1/2 cup cocoa powder

Directions:

- In a mixer with a paddle attachment, cream the butter, cream cheese and peanut butter together with the sugar until very fluffy and light. Scrape down the sides of the bowl several times to ensure all the ingredients are being mixed
- Slowly add the milk to the mixer, scraping down the bowl again to prevent clumps.
- Add the vanilla and salt and cocoa powder and mix until smooth.

– Use immediately or store at room temperature for 2 days or in the refrigerator for 6 days.

Peanut Butter Buttercream

A sweet and rich buttercream recipe for any peanut butter lover. The addition of cream cheese makes this frosting even more amazingly creamy and adds just the right amount of tang.

Yield: Frosting for 24 cupcakes or one 6" Cake

Active Time: 15 minutes

Ingredients:

- 1 cup Butter
- 1 cup Peanut Butter
- 1/2 cup Cream Cheese
- 2 Tablespoons Milk
- 4 cups Powdered Sugar
- 2 teaspoons Vanilla
- 1/4 teaspoon Salt

Directions

- In a mixer with a paddle attachment, cream the butter, cream cheese and peanut butter together with the sugar until very fluffy and light. Scrape down the sides of the bowl several times to ensure all the ingredients are being mixed
- Slowly add the milk to the mixer, scraping down the bowl again to prevent clumps.
- Add the vanilla and salt
- Use immediately or store at room temperature for 2 days or in the refrigerator for 6 days.

Peanut Butter Banana Cupcakes

Peanut butter buttercream tops this dense banana cake for a combination you won't be able to resist. Try drizzling these beauties with some chocolate sauce for an even more delightful dessert.

Yield: 24 Cupcakes

Active Time: 40 minutes

Banana Cake Ingredients:

- 1/2 cup butter, softened
- 1 1/2 cup sugar
- 2 Eggs
- 2 teaspoons Vanilla
- 1 1/2 teaspoon Baking Soda
- 1/2 teaspoon Salt
- 3/4 cups buttermilk
- 2 Cups Flour
- 2 teaspoons Lemon Juice
- 1 cup Mashed Bananas
- 1 Batch Cream Cheese Frosting (See Above)

Directions:

- In a mixer with a paddle attachment, cream the butter and sugar until fluffy and light, scraping down the sides of the bowl as needed to fully mix
- Slowly add the eggs, scraping down the bowl after each addition.
- In a separate bowl, mix the flour, baking soda, and salt. Alternated adding the dry ingredients and the buttermilk to the mixer, again scraping down the bowl as needed

- Add the mashed bananas last and mix until everything is fully combined.
- Using an ice cream scoop or a large spoon, scoop the batter into a lined cupcake pan so that the cupcake liners are halfway full. Bake at 350 ℉ for 2024 minutes then allow the cupcakes to cool in the pan.

Peanut Butter Buttercream:

- 1 cup Butter
- 1 cup Peanut Butter
- 1/2 cup Cream Cheese
- 2 Tablespoons Milk
- 4 cups Powdered Sugar
- 2 teaspoons Vanilla
- 1/4 teaspoon Salt

- In a mixer with a paddle attachment, cream the butter, cream cheese and peanut butter together with the sugar until very fluffy and light. Scrape down the sides of the bowl several times to ensure all the ingredients are being mixed
- Slowly add the milk to the mixer, scraping down the bowl again to prevent clumps.

- Add the vanilla and salt

- Using a piping bag with a large star tip, pipe the Peanut Butter Buttercream onto the cooled cupcakes. Garnish with a drizzle of chocolate sauce, mini chocolate chips or leave plain and serve immediately or store at room temperature for 2 days or in the refrigerator for 4 days.

Chocolate Peanut Butter Cupcakes

A rich, dense, chocolate cupcake filled with delicious peanut butter. Get ready to be full and so happy after one bite…but proceed to finish the rest of the cupcake!

Yield: 36 cupcakes

Active Time: 50 minutes

Chocolate Cupcakes Ingredients:

- 3 1/2 cups Flour
- 3 1/2 cups sugar
- 3 1/4 cups Cocoa Powder
- 1 Tablespoon Baking Soda
- 3/4 teaspoon baking Powder
- 1/3 teaspoon salt
- 1 1/2 cups buttermilk
- 3 eggs
- 1 1/2 cups coffee
- 3/4 cup oil
- 1 1/2 teaspoons Vanilla
- 1/2 cup peanut butter

Directions:

- In a mixer with a whisk attachment, combine all the dry ingredients and mix.
- In a separate bowl, mix the buttermilk, eggs, vanilla and oil. Slowly add this mixture to the dries, scraping down the bowl as needed.
- Lastly, add the coffee. The mix will be more liquid than a regular cake batter but that is okay!

- Using an ice cream scoop or a large spoon, scoop the batter into a lined cupcake pan so that the cupcake liners are halfway full. Bake at 350 F for 2024 minutes then allow the cupcakes to cool in the pan.
- Once the cupcakes have cooled, use an apple corer to remove the center of the cupcake by sticking it straight into the center of the cupcakes, pulling out the cake.
- Fill the center hole of the cupcakes with the peanut butter, you can either use a spoon to put the peanut butter into the hole or a piping bag will also work great and be a little less sticky.
- Ice the cupcakes with peanut butter buttercream or chocolate peanut butter buttercream for an extra rich cupcake

Chocolate Peanut Butter Bread Pudding

So, delicious and so rich, this recipe will certainly satisfy your sweet tooth! Rich chocolate, filling peanut butter and tasty bread pudding

Yield: 16 servings

Active Time: 30 minutes

Ingredients:

- 1 1/2 cups Brown Sugar
- 1 1/2 Cups Sugar
- 3 cups Whole Milk
- 7 Eggs
- 8 teaspoons Vanilla
- 9 cups cubed bread
- 1 cup Chocolate Chips
- 1/2 cup peanut butter

Directions:

- In a very large bowl, whisk the sugars and eggs together by hand. Add the peanut butter and whisk to combine
- Add the milk and vanilla to the bowl and whisk all together.
- Add the cubed bread and stir together, let the mix sit for at least an hour to allow the bread to soak up the milk mixture.
- Add the chocolate chips and pour the mixture into a 9x13 pan with 3 inch sides. Bake in a 350 F oven for 4550 minutes or until the bread pudding springs back when you touch the top and is no longer wet.

Super Fudgey Peanut Butter Brownies

So, packed with chocolate that these brownies are almost like eating a piece of fudge. They are super easy to make and just as easy to eat!

Active Time: 10 minutes

Yield: one 8x8 pan

Ingredients:

- 6 Tablespoons Butter
- 1/2 cup Sugar
- 2 teaspoons Vanilla
- 1 1/4 cup mini semisweet chocolate chips
- 2 eggs
- 1/4 cup peanut butter
- 1 1/2 Tablespoons Dark Cocoa Powder
- 2 Tablespoons Corn Starch
- 1/2 teaspoon Salt

Directions:

- In a small saucepan over low heat, melt the butter.
- Add the mini chocolate chips to the butter and stir to melt the chips. Whisk in the peanut butter and then remove from the heat.
- Add the vanilla and eggs to the chocolate to the saucepan and mix thoroughly.
- Sift cocoa powder and corn starch into the chocolate mix and stir
- Add the salt to the chocolate as well and mix everything together.

- Pour the brownies in to a well greased 8x8" square pan and into a 350 ℉ oven. Bake for 2025 minutes and then remove from oven. Allow the brownies to cool in the pan and then cool completely in the fridge as they will be easier to cut when very cold. Enjoy!

Rich Chocolate Peanut Butter Tart

This dessert is for true chocolate lovers only. It is fairly simple to make and will keep in the fridge for up to two weeks so you can definitely make this one ahead!

Yield: One 9" Tart

Active Time: 45 min

Chocolate Tart Shell Ingredients:

- 1 1/2 cup flour
- 3 Tablespoons Cocoa Powder
- 1/2 teaspoon salt

- 3/4 cup butter, softened
- 1/2 cup powdered sugar
- 1 egg
- 1 teaspoon Vanilla

Directions:

- In a food processor, mix the dry ingredients. Add the butter and pulse until small crumbles form.
- Add the egg and vanilla to the mixer and keep on until a dough ball forms.
- Put the dough onto a floured surface and roll until slightly larger than the tart shell. Move dough into the tart shell and press down so that it stays securely in the pan.
- Prick the dough all over with a fork to prevent it from rising while baking.
- Bake in a 350 ℉ oven for 20 minutes. Allow to cool

Peanut Butter Ganache

- 2 1/2 cups semi sweet chocolate chips
- 1/2 cup peanut butter
- 2 1/2 cups heavy cream

Ganache Directions:

- Put the chocolate chips and peanut butter in a large bowl and set aside
- In a saucepan, bring the heavy cream to a boil. When the cream begins to boil, immediately remove it from the heat and pour it over the chocolate chips.
- Whisk the chocolate, peanut butter and heavy cream together until a smooth chocolate forms.
- Pour the ganache into the cooled tart shell and put the tart into the refrigerator until set. Slice and serve!

Plantain Chips with Peanut Butter Dip

Plantains are just like bananas but have more fiber and therefore hold up better when cooked at high heats. Find them in any grocery store in the fruit section they will look like bigger bananas and are often sold as singles rather than in a bunch.

Yield: 4 servings

Active Time: 20 Minutes

Ingredients:

- 4 Plantains, green (not too ripe)
- 5 cups oil for frying
- 2 teaspoons salt
- 1 cup Plain Yogurt
- 1/2 cup Peanut butter

Directions:

- In a large saucepan, heat the oil to 325 °F
- Peel and slice the bananas very thin you can even use a peeler to help you get them extra skinny which makes for a crispier chip.
- Toss the plantain slices into the hot oil and fry for about a minute, only fry as many slices will fit in the oil in a single layer and keep turning them to fry each side.
- Remove from the oil and onto a paper towel lined dish

- In a small bowl, thoroughly mix the peanut butter and yogurt together for the dip.
- Sprinkle with salt while hot and serve immediately with the nutella dip

Carnival Peanut Butter Bananas

his dessert is similar to something you would find at a carnival or local fair. Packed with gooey marshmallows and baked in a convenient foil wrapper, these bananas are amped up and loaded with melty peanut butter goodness!

Yield: 4 Servings

Active Time: 15 minutes

Ingredients:

- 4 Bananas, peeled
- 1/4 cup mini marshmallows
- 1/4 cup mini chocolate chips
- 1/4 cup peanut butter

Directions:

- Lay 4 pieces of aluminum foil that are about double the size of the banana on a clean surface.
- Slice each banana lengthwise but do not cut all the way though, you want to just split the banana open in order to stuff it. Move each banana to the center of a piece of foil.
- Stuff each banana with chocolate chips making sure each banana has chocolate chips from top to bottom. Then, do the same with the mini marshmallows so each banana is full.
- Place the bananas and foil onto a sheet tray and under a 500 ℉ broiler for about 6 minutes or until the marshmallows begin to toast.
- Remove from the oven and spread with the peanut butter. Serve in the foil while hot!

Peanut Butter Chocolate Chip Biscotti

A deliciously rich biscotti that tastes amazing when paired with coffee or when eaten alone. Also try dunking these in hot chocolate for an extra rich treat!

Yield: 24 Biscotti

Total Time: 1 hour 15 minutes

Ingredients:

- 2 cups Flour
- 1 1/2 teaspoons cinnamon

- 1 teaspoon Baking Powder
- 1/2 teaspoon salt
- 2/3 cup Sugar
- 1/3 cup butter
- 2 eggs
- 1 teaspoon Vanilla Extract
- 1/4 cup peanut butter
- 1/2 cup chocolate chips

Directions:

- In a mixer with a paddle attachment or a large mixing bowl, mix together butter, peanut butter and sugar until creamy.
- Mix in the vanilla and eggs and beat until combined.
- In a separate bowl, combine flour, cinnamon, salt, and baking powder.
- Stir dry mix into bowl and mix until a dough forms
- Add the chocolate chips and mix until everything is thoroughly combined try not to over mix!
- Divide dough into two balls and roll into two logs about 9 inches long by three inches wide. Place the biscotti logs onto a cookie tray with foil. If the dough

is tacky, dip your hands in cold water and then shape the dough it's okay if the dough gets a little wet.

- Put the cookie tray into the oven and bake for about 30 to 40 minutes at 325 °F or until logs are a golden brown around the edges.

- Remove the biscotti from the oven and let cool for about 10 minutes before cutting the logs into slices about 3/4 of an inch wide. You can choose to cut the logs straight however they are typically cut diagonally.

- Put the biscotti slices back onto the sheet tray with the cut side facing up. Lower the oven temperature to 250 °F and toast the biscotti for about 8 to 10 minutes. Enjoy!

Milk Chocolate Peanut Butter Swirl Ice Cream

Not quite as heavy as regular chocolate ice cream, milk chocolate ice cream is a creamy treat that is a step up from plain vanilla. A versatile flavor that can pair with almost any dessert!

Yield: 8 Servings

Active Time: 30 minutes

Ingredients:

- 6 ounces milk chocolate
- 5 egg yolks
- 3/4 cup Sugar
- 1/4 teaspoon Salt
- 4 1/2 cups half and half
- 1 teaspoon Vanilla
- 1 cup peanut butter

Directions:

- In a mixer with a whisk attachment, whisk the egg yolks and 1/2 cup of the sugar until thick. Turn off the mixer.
- In a saucepan, combine the salt, remaining sugar and half and half. Cook the milk over medium heat until it begins to boil and turn off the heat immediately. Whisk the milk chocolate into the hot milk until completely melted and combined
- Turn on the mixer with the egg mix and while the mixer is on, slowly pour the hot milk into the eggs. Add the vanilla extract
- Once combined, pour the entire mixture back into the saucepan and then cook over the low heat, constantly

stirring until the mixture reaches 175℉ or becomes thick enough to coat the back of a spoon.

- Pour the ice cream mix into a cold bowl and refrigerate for at least 5 hours or overnight.

- Once cool, pour the ice cream mix into an ice cream maker and churn according to the manufacturer's instructions (every machine is different so be sure to read your directions!).

- Once frozen, place the ice cream into a cold bowl and swirl in the 1 cup of peanut butter quickly so that the ice cream doesn't melt. Place plastic wrap directly on the surface of the ice cream and put it immediately in the freezer. Allow to harden for at least 4 hours and then enjoy!

Peanut Butter Stuffed Chocolate Chip Cookies

Chocolate chip cookies just got even better with a surprise peanut butter center. Biting into this cookie will give you such happiness when the gooey peanut butter combines with melted chocolate chips so mouthwatering!

Yield: 36 Cookies

Total Time: 35 Minutes

Ingredients:

- 1 cup Butter
- 2 cups brown sugar (packed)
- 2 eggs
- 1 Tablespoon Vanilla Extract
- 3 cups Flour
- 1 teaspoon Baking Soda
- 1/2 teaspoon Salt
- 3 cups chocolate chips
- 1 1/2 cups peanut butter

Directions:

- Scoop the peanut butter into 36 small balls and freeze.
- In a mixer with a paddle attachment, cream the butter and brown sugar until fluffy and light
- Add the eggs and vanilla slowly, scraping down the bowl to make sure everything is fully combined
- Add the flour, baking soda and salt and mix until the cookie dough comes together (scrape down the bowl at least once to incorporate all the ingredients)
- Add the chocolate chips at the end until just combined

- Scoop half the cookie dough into small balls and put onto a foil lined sheet pan. Press a frozen peanut butter ball into the center of the cookie dough and then top with another scoop of cookie dough to completely cover the peanut butter center.
- Bake in a 350°F oven for 1516 minutes or until the edges brown and the cookie centers are just set.

Peanut Butter Hot Cocoa

What makes a warm cup of hot cocoa even better? Peanut Butter! So, rich, this drink is a dessert on its own and will be sure to warm you up on cold days.

Yield: 4 cups or cocoa

Total Time: 10 minutes

Ingredients:

- 4 cups of whole milk
- 4 packets of hot cocoa mix
- 1/2 cup peanut butter
- 1/2 cup mini marshmallows

Directions:

- In a medium sized saucepan, bring the milk to a boil.
- Add the peanut butter and hot cocoa mix and stir until combined.
- Pour into 4 mugs and top with marshmallows. Serve immediately while hot!

Mocha and Peanut Butter Latte

When you need coffee, chocolate and peanut butter in the morning, then this recipe is perfect for you! If you do not have an espresso machine, simply substitute the espresso for strong coffee and steam some milk in a microwave or stovetop to get the same delicious flavors.

Active Time: 10 minutes

Yield: 1 Latte

Ingredients:

- 1 shot of espresso
- 1 cup whole milk
- 2 Tablespoons peanut butter
- 1 Tablespoon cocoa powder

Directions:

- In a small saucepan or using a steam wand on an espresso machine, heat the milk to almost boiling.
- Stir in the cocoa powder and peanut butter until completely combined in the milk.
- Add the espresso and pour into a mug. Enjoy!

Peanut Butter Cookies

This amazing recipe gives you a classic, delicious peanut butter cookie. No frills needed, just perfect peanut butter goodness.

Yield: 24 Cookies

Time: 30 minutes

Ingredients:

- 1 cup butter
- 1 1/4 cup Peanut Butter
- 1 cup Sugar
- 1 cup Brown Sugar
- 2 Eggs

- 2 1/2 cup Flour
- 1 teaspoon Baking Powder
- 1/2 teaspoon Salt
- 1 teaspoon Vanilla

Directions:

- In a mixer with a paddle attachment, cream the butter, peanut butter, sugar and brown sugar until fluffy and light, scraping down the bowl several times
- Add the eggs and vanilla and scrape the bowl down again, making sure everything is thoroughly mixed.
- Add all the dry ingredients to the bowl and mix until a dough forms.
- Scoop cookie dough onto a greased cookie sheet about 2 inches apart and bake in a 350 F oven for 1012 minutes or until the edges start to brown. Cool and Enjoy!

Peanut Butter and Greens Smoothie

This smoothie is loaded with things that are so good for you. It is just an extra plus that it tastes so good! Chocolate, Peanut Butter and veggies? You've gotta try it to become a believer.

Yield: 1 smoothie

Active Time: 5 minutes

Ingredients:

- 1 banana
- 1 1/2 cup baby spinach

- 1 cup almond milk
- 2 tablespoons peanut butter
- 1 tablespoon cocoa powder
- 3 tablespoons honey
- 1/4 teaspoon ground cinnamon

Directions:

- Place all of the ingredients into a blender and puree until smooth.
- Serve and Drink immediately!

Peanut Butter Chocolate Chip Cookies

These amazing cookies combine the classic peanut butter cookie with the perfect amount of chocolate chips making them hard to resist. If you love peanut butter cookies and chocolate chip cookies, then these are sure to be your new favorite!

Yield: 24 Cookies

Time: 30 minutes

Ingredients:

- 1 cup butter
- 1 1/4 cup Peanut Butter
- 1 cup Sugar
- 1 cup Brown Sugar
- 2 Eggs
- 2 1/2 cup Flour
- 1 teaspoon Baking Powder
- 1/2 teaspoon Salt
- 1 teaspoon Vanilla
- 1 cup mini chocolate chips

Directions:

- In a mixer with a paddle attachment, cream the butter, peanut butter, sugar and brown sugar until fluffy and light, scraping down the bowl several times
- Add the eggs and vanilla and scrape the bowl down again, making sure everything is thoroughly mixed.
- Add all the dry ingredients to the bowl and mix until a dough forms.
- Add the mini chocolate chips to the dough and mix until combined

- Scoop cookie dough onto a greased cookie sheet about 2 inches apart and bake in a 350℉ oven for 1012 minutes or until the edges start to brown. Cool and Enjoy!

Spicy Peanut Sauce

This sauce is great on chicken especially when you are grilling. You can also try it as a coating for chicken wings! A deliciously thick, creamy and tangy sauce.

Yield: Sauce for 1 pound of chicken

Active Time: 5 minutes

Ingredients:

- 1/2 cup peanut butter, smooth
- 1/2 teaspoon red pepper flakes
- 1 clove garlic, minced
- 1 teaspoon salt
- 1/2 teaspoon cumin
- 1 lemon, juiced
- 1/2 cup water

Directions:

- In a medium bowl, combine all of the ingredients and whisk together until smooth.
- Use the sauce as a marinade for chicken or save it and slather it on cooked chicken. This sauce also makes a great dip!

Peanut Butter Dressing

While this may sound a little too heavy for a salad, it is actually the perfect compliment for Asian style dishes. Simple enough to make and loaded with flavor, you can't go wrong with this recipe.

Yield: Dressing for 23 salads

Active Time: 5 minutes

Ingredients:

- 1/4 cup smooth peanut butter
- 1 tablespoon coconut aminos
- 1 1/2 tablespoon rice wine vinegar
- 1 tablespoon sesame seeds
- 1/2 teaspoon red pepper flakes

Directions:

– Whisk all of the ingredients together in a medium sized bowl until smooth.
– Refrigerate until needed and serve with Asian style salads

Peanut Butter Dog Cookies

You never want to leave out your dog! These peanut butter treats are sure to go quickly and maybe you'll even get a big, wet dog kiss!

Yield: 30 dog treats

Total Time: 30 minutes

Ingredients:

- 2 cups Flour
- 1 teaspoon Baking Powder
- 1 cup Peanut Butter
- 3/4 cup milk

Directions:

- Put peanut butter in a mixer with a paddle attachment and slowly add the milk to combine
- Add the baking powder and flour to the peanut butter mix and mix until the dough just comes together
- Roll dough on floured surface to 1/8" thick
- Cut into desired shape (ask your dog what he likes best!)
- Bake in a 325 °F oven for 15 minutes and allow to cool before serving them to your pet!

Banana Cake with peanut Butter Chips

A dense and sweet cake that is a great use for brown bananas the browner the better! This goes great with peanut butter or chocolate icing for a very rich dessert.

Yield: 2 8" Round Cake Pans

Active Time: 20 minutes

Ingredients:

- 1/2 cup of butter, softened
- 1 1/2 cup sugar
- 2 teaspoons Vanilla
- 1 1/2 teaspoon of Baking Soda
- 1/2 teaspoon Salt
- 3/4 cups buttermilk
- 2 Eggs
- 2 teaspoons Lemon Juice
- 2 Cups Flour
- 1 cup Mashed Bananas
- 2 cups peanut butter chips

Directions:

- In a mixer with a paddle attachment, mix to cream the butter and sugar until fluffy and light, scraping down the sides of the bowl as needed to fully mix
- Slowly add the eggs. Be sure to scrape down the bowl after each addition.
- In a separate bowl, mix the flour, baking soda, and salt. Alternated adding the buttermilk and the dry

ingredients to the mixer, again scraping down the bowl as needed

– Add the mashed bananas and peanut butter chips and mix until everything is fully combined

– Pour the batter evenly into two 8 inch cake pans that have been greased and lined with a parchment circle in the bottom. Bake the cakes in a 350 F oven for 4050 minutes until the center of the cakes are firm to the touch.

– Allow cakes to cool in the pan before flipping them out onto a cooling rack. Ice as desired and enjoy!

Peanut Butter Banana Bread

This recipe is best when using old bananas that's right, dark brown, almost black bananas! If you have browning bananas but you aren't quite ready to use them, peel them and freeze them to use in this recipe later.

Yield: One Loaf

Active Time: 25 minutes

Ingredients:

- 1/4 cup butter
- 1/4 cup peanut butter
- 1/2 cup brown sugar
- 1/4 cup sugar

- 2 eggs
- 4 bananas, peeled
- 2 cups flour
- 1 teaspoon baking soda
- 2 teaspoons cinnamon
- 1/2 teaspoon salt

Directions:

- In a mixer with a paddle attachment, cream the butter, peanut butter, sugar and brown sugar. Scrape down the bowl several times until everything is combined and the mix is fluffy and light
- Add the eggs to the mixer and scrape down the sides of the bowl to fully incorporated.
- Add the peeled bananas and mix
- Add the flour, baking soda, cinnamon and salt and mix until a smooth batter forms
- Pour the batter into a greased loaf pan and bake at 350 °F for 4555 minutes or until the center is firm and springs back to the touch.
- Allow the bread to cool in the pan for 15 minutes and then flip onto a cooling rack. Wrap and store at the

room temperature for up to a week or can be frozen
for up to three months.

Peanut Butter Snack Mix

Sweet and salty, peanut buttery and practically irresistible, you will crave this snack mix after just one bite. Once you make this mix once, you will need to again and again!

Yield: 8 Servings

Active Time: 20 minutes

Ingredients:

- 10 cups Rice Chex cereal
- 1 1/2 cups mini chocolate chips
- 3/4 cup smooth peanut butter
- 2 teaspoons vanilla
- 1/2 stick butter, melted
- 2 teaspoons salt
- 2 cups sifted powdered sugar
- 2 cups salted peanuts
- 2 cups pretzels
- 1 cup Chocolate Chips
- 1 cup peanut butter chips

Directions:

- In a large bowl, melt the chocolate, peanut butter and salt together over a double boiler. Whisk together until smooth.
- Whisk in the melted butter and vanilla once off the heat
- Place the chex cereal in a very large bowl and pour the melted chocolate mix over the cereal. Mix together well to make sure the cereal is completely coated in the chocolate mix.

- Let the cereal cool for about 5 minutes and then transfer to a new large bowl.
- Toss the powdered sugar into the bowl with the chocolate coated cereal and mix together so that the sugar coats the cereal completely.
- Spread the cereal onto a sheet pan and let cool for about 2 hours before breaking into smaller pieces (the cereal will stick together so you will want to try to break it back into small, bite size sections).
- Add the pretzels, chocolate chips, peanut butter chips and peanuts to the cereal and mix everything well. Serve and enjoy!

Peanut Butter and Jelly Oat Bites

These little raspberry bites and peanut butter bites are loaded with flavor and so easy to make. The oat crumble is the perfect topping to these delicious little squares.

Active Time: 20 minutes

Yield: 24 squares

Ingredients:

- 1/3 cup brown sugar
- 1/2 cup butter (softened)
- 1 cup Flour
- 1/4 teaspoon Baking Soda
- 1/4 teaspoon Salt
- 3/4 cups Rolled Oats
- 1/2 cup smooth peanut butter
- 1/2 cup Raspberry Jam

Directions:

- In a mixer with a paddle attachment, combine the brown sugar and butter and mix until combined, smooth and fluffy.
- Add the flour, baking soda, salt and rolled oats to the sugar mix and turn the mixer on low until crumbles start to form. Try not to over mix the dough to prevent it from becoming tough. Turn the mixer off when the crumbles just start to form
- Preheat the oven to 350°F and grease or line a 9 x 13 pan with parchment

- Put half of the dough crumbles into the pan and push the dough into the pan using your hands or a small rolling pin.
- Spread the peanut butter onto the dough in the pan and using a small offset spatula and then spread the jam on top of the peanut butter. Make sure both the peanut butter and the jelly go all the way to the edges of the pan and completely cover the crust.
- Sprinkle the remaining dough crumbles over the top of the jam, distributing it evenly.
- Bake the bars in the preheated oven for about 30 minutes or until the crumble begins to turn golden.
- Allow the bars to cool and then cut into 1 by 1 inch squares.

Peanut Butter Truffles

An easy and impressive truffle that everyone will rave about. These make great gifts as long as you make them right before gifting they only keep for about 2 weeks in the fridge!

Yield: About 15 truffles

Active Time: 15 minutes

Ingredients:

- 2 cups peanut butter, smooth or crunchy will work
- 2 bananas, mashed
- 2 tablespoons ground flaxseeds
- 1/2 teaspoon vanilla
- 1/4 teaspoon salt
- 1 1/2 tablespoons cocoa powder

Directions:

- In a medium sized bowl, combine the vanilla, peanut butter, bananas, salt and flax seeds and mix together until smooth.
- Scoop into small balls and roll with your hands to make the balls smooth.
- Toss the rolled balls in the cocoa powder and coat them completely.
- Store in an airtight container in the fridge for up to two weeks for a yummy healthy dessert.

Peanut Butter Apple Oatmeal

A delicious and healthy way to start your day! Sweetened with honey and packed with goodness, this oatmeal should become part of your daily routine.

Yield: 2 servings

Active Time: 10 minutes

Ingredients:

- 2 cups rolled oats
- 4 1/2 cups almond milk
- 1 medium apple, diced
- 3 tablespoons peanut butter
- 3 tablespoons honey
- 1 tablespoon ground flaxseeds
- 1/2 teaspoon cinnamon
- 1/2 teaspoon vanilla

Directions:

- In a medium sized pan, bring the almond milk to a boil. Add the oats, diced apple, peanut butter, honey, flaxseeds, cinnamon and vanilla to the pan and lower the heat so the mixture is just simmering.
- Simmer for 5 minutes, stirring occasionally.
- Serve while hot!

Peanut Butter Milkshake

Peanut butter and ice cream there is no better combo! Whip up this quick tasty dessert anytime you need a peanut butter and ice cream fix.

Yield: 1 milkshake

Active Time: 5 minutes

Ingredients:

- 1/2 cup milk
- 2 cups vanilla ice cream
- 4 tablespoons smooth peanut butter

- 2 teaspoons ground flaxseeds
- 1/2 teaspoon vanilla
- 1/4 teaspoon salt

Directions:

- Scoop all of the ingredients into a blender.
- Blend until smooth and pour into a large cup
- Enjoy while cold!

Hot and Tangy Peanut Dip

This is a great dip to serve with crackers or a nice crusty bread. The peanut butter gives it a nice thick texture while the peppers add a flavorful spicy kick.

Active Time: 10 minutes

Yield: About 6 servings

Ingredients:

- 1/2 cup smooth peanut butter
- 2 jalapenos, stem and seeds removed
- 1 clove garlic
- Juice from 1 lime
- 4 tablespoons apple cider
- 2 tablespoons soy sauce

Directions:

- Place all of the ingredients in a food processor or blender.
- Blend until nice and smooth. If the dip is too thick, add a little more apple juice until it is the consistency you would like.
- Serve immediately or store in an air tight container for up to 2 weeks.

Peanut Noodles

A super easy way to have an Asian inspired meal in a hurry. You probably already have most of these ingredients at home so whip up some of these tasty noodles for dinner!

Yield: 4 Servings

Active Time: 10 minutes

Ingredients:

- One box (10 oz.) spaghetti
- 5 tablespoons peanut butter, smooth (not chunky)
- 2 tablespoons rice wine vinegar
- 2 tablespoons soy sauce
- 1/2 cup minced scallions
- 1/4 teaspoon salt
- 1/2 teaspoon black pepper

Directions:

- Make the pasta according to the directions on the box. When straining the pasta, keep 1/2 cup of the pasta water.
- In a medium sized bowl, whisk together the pasta water and all the remaining ingredients. Whisk until nice and smooth.
- Toss the pasta in the peanut sauce and serve while hot!

Peanut Butter Belgian Waffles

A super hearty waffle that adds some great flavor and protein to your breakfast. Top these waffles with some jelly and you'll have a new twist on a PB&J!

Yield: 8 servings

Active Time: 15 minutes

Ingredients:

- 1 3/4 cups flour
- 1 Tablespoon of baking powder
- 4 tablespoons granulated sugar
- 1 teaspoons salt
- 2 eggs, lightly whisked
- 1 1/2 cups milk
- 1/4 cup vegetable oil
- 1 teaspoon vanilla extract
- 1/4 cup peanut butter

Directions:

- In a medium sized bowl, whisk together the all of dry ingredients (flour, baking powder, sugar and salt).
- In a separate small bowl, whisk all of the wet ingredients together (the milk, vegetable oil, eggs, and vanilla).
- Add about 1/4 of the wet mixture to the peanut butter in a new bowl and whisk until the peanut butter is smooth. Add the remaining wet ingredients to the peanut butter bowl, whisking constantly to ensure the peanut butter if fully combined and doesn't clump.

- Slowly add wet ingredients to the dries, whisking constantly so that no lumps form. (If you do have any lumps, use a rubber spatula to try to press them against the side of the bowl and break them up.)
- Heat your waffle maker according to your manufacturer's directions.
- Cook the batter according to your waffle makers directions every machine is slightly different regarding cooking time! Enjoy these waffles while they are still hot alone or paired with your favorite toppings

Chocolate Peanut Butter Waffles

The chocolate and peanut butter combination is hard to resist and these waffles will be too! The Chopped Reese's peanut butter cups are just the icing on the cake or the perfect topping on the waffle!!

Yield: 8 servings

Active Time: 15 minutes

Ingredients:

- 1 3/4 cups flour
- 1 Tablespoon of baking powder
- 1/4 cup cocoa powder
- 5 tablespoons granulated sugar
- 1 teaspoons salt
- 2 eggs, lightly whisked
- 1/4 cup peanut butter
- 1 1/2 cups milk
- 1/4 cup vegetable oil
- 2 teaspoon vanilla extract
- 1/2 cup chopped reese's peanut butter cups

Directions:

- In a medium sized bowl, whisk together the all of dry ingredients (flour, baking powder, sugar, cocoa powder and salt).
- In a separate small bowl, whisk all of the wet ingredients together (the milk, vegetable oil, eggs, and vanilla).
- Add about 1/4 of the wet mixture to the peanut butter in a new bowl and whisk until the peanut butter is smooth. Add the remaining wet ingredients to the

peanut butter bowl, whisking constantly to ensure the peanut butter if fully combined and doesn't clump.

- Slowly add wet ingredients to the dries, whisking constantly so that no lumps form. (If you do have any lumps, use a rubber spatula to try to press them against the side of the bowl and break them up.)

- Heat your waffle maker according to your manufacturer's directions.

- Cook the batter according to your waffle makers directions every machine is slightly different regarding cooking time! Top with chopped peanut butter cups and serve while hot.

Made in the USA
Middletown, DE
27 November 2018